NATURE GOT MAD

RICKY CLEMONS

PUBLISHED BY FIEDLI PUBLISHING, INC.

Copyright ©2021, Ricky Clemons

ALL RIGHTS RESERVED.

No part of this publication may be reproduced, stored in a retrieval system, or transmitted in any form or by any means—electronic, mechanical, photo-copy, recording, or any other—except for brief quotation in reviews, without the prior permission of the author or publisher.

ISBN: 978-1-60414-910-4

Published by

Fideli Publishing, Inc.
119 W. Morgan St.
Martinsville, IN 46151
www.FideliPublishing.com

Table of Contents

Nature Got Mad 1
I Had Lost My Mind 6
Getting an Education 12
Then What About a Human Being? 14
Our Valley Shepherd 16
Keep a Watch on Our Hearts 19
No Matter How 22
Who is Forevermore 27
Under the Sun 30
The Moonlight Glow of Time 33
A Lot of People 36
You Can Only Live Your Life 41
I Want to Help People Make it to Heaven 43
A Spiritual Birthday 45
Don't Judge People 47
The Lord Amazes Me 49
Many People Know Better 51
I Can Always 53
The More 55
All Around The World 56
There Are People Who Believe 58
Holy Word, O Lord 60

In Jesus' Hands 62

By the Choices We Make 64

Living by Faith 66

The Pandemic of Sin 68

Stand Up and Pick Up Your Mat 70

Fear Can Be a Good Thing 72

Many People Don't Believe 74

Higher 76

There is Something New to Learn 78

It's Easy to Think About 80

To Tell Everything 82

We Can Limp Spiritually 84

If You Know It All 86

I Had Completely Forgotten 88

Will One Day Be Immortal 90

Nature Knows Our Black Struggles 92

Poetry About the Lord 97

Out of Our Comfort Zone 99

Nature Got Mad

Nature got mad at those two teenaged boys who sexually assaulted me when I was a little boy.

They sexually assaulted me in the backyard outhouse.

They sexually assaulted me more than once.

That terrible, degrading act gave me a dim outlook on life.

I felt so ashamed of myself for many years and I did not tell anyone what happened to me.

This forever changed my life in my early childhood years.

My life had suddenly changed in some dark ways that I did not understand.

Those two teenaged boys had befriended my family, but my family just didn't know what they did to me.

After what happened to me, I wasn't that little happy boy anymore.

As I grew up, I lived my life as if I was never sexually assaulted, and that caused me to wander through life with no real meaning or idea of who I was.

I would get into fights, and just didn't care at all.

When no one knew what had happened to me, nature knew what had happened and got mad at those two teenaged boys.

Nature was my witness when I felt so all alone and so ashamed that I covered it up for years and years.

I would make friends, but I had no real trust and couldn't get close to them.

When I grew up to be a man, I joined the Army and wanted to prove to myself that I could be a man of war and fight in battles.

I never got a chance to do that though, because I got ill from using illegal drugs.

I got well trained in being a combat soldier in basic training.

I was ready to take on anything that came my way, but sadly I wasn't trained to protect myself from those two teenaged boys who sexually assaulted me when I was a little boy.

I don't ever remember crying about what happened to me.

I was so angry that I hid what had happened from my family, because I just didn't know how to express it in a civilized way.

I turned to a promiscuous lifestyle.

I had girlfriends I used for sex.

I had some one-night stands with different women.

I knew that my bad behavior all stemmed from the sexual assault that was done to me.

I was in and out of relationships with the women who came into my life.

I was terribly wounded in my soul and pretended that I was all right and that it was okay to use those women for sex.

This was my way of escaping my pain that was like a leech sucking the blood out of my body.

I also drank alcohol and smoked cigarettes, but that could not heal my pain.

For years and years, I wondered why I was left all alone to be assaulted.

I felt like my life was a dry well.

I felt like my life was broken glass.

I felt like my life was a faded picture in a frame.

I felt like my life was sand running out of an hourglass.

I felt like my life was a toothache.

I felt like my life was a dusty book on a shelf.

I felt like my life was a big hole in the wall.

I felt like my life was garbage.

I felt like my life was a bad accident.

I felt like my life was a big lie.

I felt like my life was nothing.

When I was sexually assaulted, my whole life changed and I felt like the most filthy carpet that anyone could walk on.

That is what I felt like when I was sexually assaulted by those two boys who were brothers.

It was bad enough to get sexually assaulted by one person, but when it was two people at the same time, even nature wept bitterly.

Nature was mad and I was numb and did not understand how I felt after I was sexually assaulted.

Today, I truly thank Jesus Christ that it wasn't worse than what it was.

Since I've given my life to Jesus, He uses my pain to make me strong so that I can encourage others who have been sexually assaulted and let them know it is not their fault.

Jesus has turned my pain into great strength so that I can write this and share it with others so that they can know that their lives are not a dead end.

Those two teenaged boys sinned against God when they did what they did to me.

They also committed a terrible crime that they got away with.

Today, I am at peace with myself and my Lord Jesus Christ who says that vengeance is His.

My hope Is that my sexual abusers have confessed and repented of their sins unto the Lord and turned away from living in darkness.

What they did to me gives me no excuse to live my life in any kind of way against the Lord, who has brought me this far in my right mind so that I can write this to help strengthen others so they can overcome their trauma from being sexually assaulted.

Nature is mad at those two teenaged boys who sexually assaulted me.

But, nature is happy to see me doing as well as I am in Jesus' name.

Nature knew that when I gave my heart to Jesus, my life would change.

The Lord gave me a treasure chest of poetry to write about Him.

Nature knew that when I gave my heart to Jesus, my life would change.

The Lord gave me an overflow of poetry about Him.

Nature got mad, but is smiling today because I gave my myself to Jesus when my trauma from my sexual assault tried to destroy my life.

Those two teenaged boys sexually assaulted my body, but they could not sexually assault my choice and keep me from making Jesus Christ my Savior.

Those two teenaged boys sexually assaulted my body, but they could not sexually assault my heart and keep me from being saved in Jesus Christ today.

Nature got mad, but will never regret that Jesus used my trauma from my sexual assault to fix me up and make me whole so that I can serve others with my life and my ministry of poetry that is not finished until Jesus says that it is finished.

When I was sexually assaulted, that was the root of a lot of my problems in my life.

That angry part of me died when I gave my life to Jesus Christ.

Nature cried out to God in its madness and asked Jesus to keep me safe and see me through this sexual assault.

Many people have been sexually assaulted.

They feel ashamed and they don't want to talk about it or write about it or shared with others and be transparent.

Nature is always transparent and gives you and me real tranquility in a troubled world.

Nature will get mad at people who don't care who they hurt.

Nature is always true to stay in its place and treat you and me right each day.

Nature got mad and didn't sin against God when Nature witnessed me being sexually assaulted.

God is seen in nature and that teaches me how to be transparent, even when bad influences are trying to corrupt my soul.

When Nature saw those corrupt acts of those two teenaged boys sexually assaulting me, Nature got mad.

Nature asked God to keep those corrupt acts from corrupting me so that I would not do to others what was done to me.

I am so thankful to God today that no one can say that I caused nature to get mad at me.

Nature would not ever convince God to be against me.

I thank Jesus Christ, my Lord, for giving me the strength to write about my sexual assault.

I am sharing my past with others who may be able to relate to what I have been through.

I want to let them know that the Lord can use this type of bad experience to strengthen them, just like He strengthened me.

I Had Lost My Mind

It began when I took some leave time from my military duty and went home.

I took my thirty days of leave time to go back home and spend time with my kinfolks and girlfriend.

I surely spent most of my time with my girlfriend, and I smoked some marijuana with her.

I bought some marijuana from a man I knew and trusted.

Before that, I had bought marijuana and had been smoking some at my permanent duty station in Hawaii.

I was smoking some good marijuana in Hawaii.

That marijuana didn't give me any bad side effects, even though I knew that it was wrong for me to smoke it.

The marijuana I bought from the man I knew back in my hometown was some marijuana that was bad to smoke.

I smoked it anyway, and it caused me to feel good, so I shared it with my girlfriend.

During my thirty days of leave time, I was smoking a lot of marijuana.

One day, I felt funny and I had a feeling like I had never had before.

My leave time was finished and it was time for me to pack up and travel back to my permanent duty station in Hawaii.

I was in the 25th Infantry Division at the Schofield barracks.

I was in the 65th Engineer Battalion in the Army.

I was young and proud of being in the Army.

When I got back to the barracks I lived in with the other soldiers, I felt that funny feeling a lot more and it was getting stronger.

I felt like everyone could see right through me and could read my mind.

I began to isolate myself by staying in my room and not going anywhere.

I had no appetite at all and didn't eat anything.

I lost so much weight that I was absent from some of my formations in the squad.

I just didn't know what was going on with me.

My company Commander ordered all the soldiers in the company to go to the Big Island on a mission for one month.

I had to go, regardless of how I felt.

I had never thought about seeing a doctor before going to the Big Island.

When I got to the Big Island, I still felt so strange around the other soldiers but I found the strength to perform my duties.

One weekend, some other soldiers and I got together to go to one of the towns on the Big Island.

When we got there, we met some young native women and smoked marijuana with them and drank some alcohol.

By this time after spending so much time alone, I had lost a lot of my social skills, but I still hung out with them that weekend.

My 30-day mission was completed on the Big Island, and I didn't feel any different from how I felt before I went there.

As I got back to the barracks, I began to isolate myself again.

One day, I was standing out on the balcony in the barracks and one of my soldier friends who was from New York said to me, "You are not the same as you used to be."

He also said that I needed to see a doctor.

I took his advice and put in for sick leave from my duties.

When I visited the doctor, the doctor asked me some questions about how I was feeling.

I told the doctor how I was feeling, and before I knew what was going on, the doctor had admitted me to the hospital and put me on some medication.

I was in the hospital for some months, and my squad leader visited me to see if I was well enough to come back and perform my duty.

That never happened though, because I was transferred to another hospital in Washington, DC.

I didn't realize that I'd had a nervous breakdown and the marijuana I smoked had been the cause.

One of my doctors told me that I would never be able to socialize again.

I know today that it was Jesus Christ who blessed the medicine to help my mind to heal so that I could live a normal life today.

Jesus proved that doctor wrong when he told me that I would never socialized again.

Thanks to Jesus Christ, I can socialize with people again.

I was discharged from the Army with a medical honorable discharge.

Thanks to the Lord, I was still able to work some jobs.

Today, I am living my life unto the Lord, who has blessed me to overcome my drug addiction.

The Lord has blessed me to be able to socialize with people.

The Lord has blessed me to express myself, even in the poetry that I love to write about my Lord Jesus Christ.

My nervous breakdown caused me to have some memory loss.

My memory is not so good, but I am thankful unto the Lord that my memory is as good as it is because I am able to have the knowledge to write poetry about the Lord.

When I lost my mind, the devil meant it for my bad but the Lord used it for my good so I could help encourage others and show them that there is nothing the Lord can't do for them.

I think about King Nebuchadnezzar who lost his mind for seven years.

God restored his mind, even though God had caused him to lose it in the first place because Nebuchadnezzar had wanted people to worship him like he was God.

No matter what caused me to lose my mind, I am so glad that the Lord God has restored my mind.

I know that I don't deserve this because I was living in sin against God, who showed me His mercy.

Thanks to Jesus Christ, today the devil doesn't make me smoke marijuana and use illegal drugs anymore.

No human being made me smoke that marijuana and use illegal drugs.

I am to blame, and today I own up to it because the Lord showed me that I must answer to Him alone.

Whether I caused myself to have a mental breakdown or not, the Lord has brought me this far and restored my mind through some good medicine.

The Lord is still using that medicine today to help me to live a good, normal life.

I thank my Lord and Savior Jesus Christ for sparing my life and giving me a chance to share my testimony with you about what He brought me through.

I lost my mind, but I didn't know that I had lost my mind.

I lost my mind and reality couldn't find me.

I lost my mind and time couldn't find me.

I lost my mind and I couldn't find it.

I lost my mind and no human being could find it.

Only my Lord Jesus Christ could find my lost mind, and He found it because He knew where it was.

I am so glad that Jesus gave me my mind back through the good medicine that He inspired the doctors to give to me.

In some ways, my mind is so much better today than before I lost it when I was about 19 years old and in the military.

There is nothing Jesus Christ can't do.

Jesus can make the impossible possible in my life and in your life.

Many years ago, I believed that it was impossible for me to live in reality again.

When I lost my mind, reality left me behind and I was in an unrealistic state of mind.

It was like being blind and I could not see where I was going in my life.

I know today that the Lord winked His eye at my ignorance that may have played a part in me losing my mind, because I believe that if I had not used the illegal drugs I would never have lost my mind.

I am no better than anyone else who may have lost their mind.

It's like an unsolved mystery why some people lose their minds and never get them back again.

I can't question the Lord as to why He allowed me to lose my mind many years ago when I was very young, but I am so happy today that I can see the full strength of reality in my life.

The Lord has restored my mental powers through good medicine that I still take today.

Good medicine is from the Lord, who gives scientists the wisdom and knowledge to create good medicine to help me and you get well if it is in God's will.

It was in God's will for the medicine to work for me.

God is the best doctor in the medical field all around the world every day.

God is the best psychiatrist, psychologist, surgeon, and scientist all around the world every day.

It's the Lord God who gives everyone in the medical field wisdom, knowledge, and experience to use for His glory and not to get the glory and praise for themselves.

I truly thank God for using those professional people in the medical field, even when some of those doctors, psychiatrists, psychologists, surgeons, and scientists can sometimes do people more harm than good.

God's son, Jesus Christ, is the only one who can heal our sins and our sick souls.

Having a sick soul is the worst kind of sickness in this world every day.

I had once lost my mind, but the Lord didn't let me die in my sins for my soul to be lost — that would be forevermore worse than losing my mind.

It's a miracle to me today that I am well enough in my mind to write about my bad experiences and to share them with others.

I am doing what the Lord wants me to do, which is to help others who may not understand what it's like to lose your mind.

I am doing what the Lord wants me to do by not judging those who have lost their minds.

I didn't ever think that I would lose my mind, but it happened to me.

Today, though, I am a living miracle because of my Lord Jesus Christ.

Getting an Education

Getting an education is learning to acquire knowledge that can prosper you in this world.

Getting an education is accumulating a lot of information for your well-being and the well-being of others.

Getting an education is learning a lot of things so you can survive in this world.

Getting an education is expanding your mind with above-average things.

Getting an education is filling up your mind with knowledge.

Getting an education is taking your mind beyond common sense.

Getting an education is learning what is right and what is wrong.

Getting an education is making this world a better place to live in.

Getting an education is learning how to solve problems.

Getting an education is learning how to thoroughly communicate with people and understand them.

Getting an education is sharing your knowledge.

Getting an education is learning how to not be ignorant.

Getting an education is learning how to connect with people.

Getting an education is getting knowledge to teach the feeble-minded people.

Getting an education is reaching up to a higher intelligence.

Getting an education is learning how to increase your mental powers.

Getting a Christian education is learning how to get to know the Lord Jesus Christ.

Getting a Christian education is getting knowledge of God's holy word.

Getting a Christian education is learning how to be a witness of Jesus Christ.

Getting a Christian education is learning how to win souls to Jesus Christ.

Getting a Christian education is learning how to be a disciple of Jesus Christ.

Getting a Christian education is learning how to build up the Church of Jesus Christ.

Getting a Christian education is learning how to live right by example, so people can see Jesus in you and me.

Then What About a Human Being?

If an animal can hurt and suffer from pain, then what about a human being who can hurt, suffer from pain and talk about it?

An animal can't talk about hurt and suffering.

If an animal can starve from having no food to eat and suffer from malnutrition, then what about a human being who can starve from having no food to eat, suffer from malnutrition and talk about it?

Our hearts can hurt for an animal that's feeling pain and suffering, but what about a human being. Should our hearts hurt even more for them?

An animal can be abused and you and I can want to put the abuser in jail, but what about a human being who can be abused? You and I can want to put the abuser in jail for a long time.

An animal can get sick, and you and I can shed some tears about it, but what about a human being who can get sick? Will you and I shed some tears about them too?

An animal can die, and you and I can grieve about it, but what about a human being who dies? Will you and I grieve a lot more?

God didn't create animals in His image, but an animal can cheer us up if we are feeling down.

God didn't create animals in His image, but an animal can motivate us to do what is right.

God didn't create animals in His image, but an animal can save someone's life.

God didn't create animals in His image, but an animal can sense that something is wrong.

God didn't create animals in His image, but an animal can love you and me.

God loves all the animals that He created for His pleasure, but what about human beings who God created in His image to really see Him?

A human being can pray to God, but an animal can't pray to God.

A human being can choose to love and obey God, but an animal can't choose to love and obey God.

A human being can make choices, but an animal can't make choices.

Animals do things by their fixed pattern of behaviors, but we human beings can choose to change our behaviors.

A wild man can choose to change his behavior, but a tamed animal can't choose to change its behavior.

An animal can live a natural life, but what about a human being who can choose to be natural?

Our Valley Shepherd

Your valley to walk through may be your imprisonment.

Your valley to walk through may be your marriage.

Your valley to walk through may be yourself.

Your valley to walk through may be your desires.

You and I have a valley to walk through, and we need Jesus Christ to lead us through our valley of life.

A valley is a very low place to walk through.

It can be a depressing place to walk through.

If you and I try to walk through our valley all alone, we will get weary.

If you and I try to walk through our valley all alone, we will faint.

If you and I try to walk through our valley all alone, we will get bit by the serpent of distress.

Your valley to walk through may be your finances.

Your valley to walk through may be your reasoning.

Your valley to walk through may be your ideas.

Only Jesus can make your valley a good experience to walk through.

Jesus can make your valley worth the walk.

A valley is a low place between the hills and the mountains.

Sometimes, you and I must walk down in the valley of our life to get to the top of the hills of our problems.

Sometimes, you and I must walk down in the valley to get to the top of the mountain of our achievement.

Life is not always easy, and the valley will surely let us know that.

You and I can be very thankful that Jesus will pick us up and carry us through the valley of uncertainty that can spiritually dehydrate us.

Jesus will pick us up and carry us through the valley of life, if we trust and depend on Him.

Sometimes, you and I must walk through the valley to truly appreciate life.

Sometimes, you and I must walk through the valley to be content in life.

Sometimes, you and I must walk through the valley and humble ourselves before the Lord.

Sometimes you and I must walk through the valley and be thankful unto the Lord.

Jesus is our Valley Shepherd who walks with us through the valley of death.

Jesus is our Valley Shepherd who walks with us through the valley of the unknown.

Jesus is our Valley Shepherd who walks with us through the valley of heartache.

Jesus is our Valley Shepherd who walks with us through the valley of disappointment.

Jesus is our Valley Shepherd who walks with us through the valley of injustice.

Jesus is our Valley Shepherd and Jesus is our Mountain Shepherd who walks with us to give us the victory over our misfortunes.

There is nothing that Jesus can't do for you and me.

Jesus can do all good things for you and me so that we can walk through life and death.

Your valley may be unforgiveness.

Your valley may be jealousy.

Your valley may be prejudice.

Your valley may be lust.

Your valley may be not showing respect of other persons.

Your valley may be made of greed for worldly gain.

You and I have a valley to walk through by our free will choice.

You and I can choose to make Jesus Christ our Valley Shepherd, and He will chase away the spiritual predators and keep them from destroying you and me as we walk through the valley of the world that is low down in the rebellion against God.

Keep a Watch on Our Hearts

Only the Lord always sees our hearts and keeps a watch on our hearts.

You can't keep a watch on my heart, and I can keep a watch on your heart.

I can say one thing and do another thing.

You can say one thing and do another thing.

Only the Lord always knows our hearts and keeps a watch on our hearts every day.

I can write all the poems that I want to write about the Lord.

All of my poems are not what is in my whole heart that the Lord keeps a watch on.

The Lord sees all of my motives.

The Lord sees all of my intentions.

The Lord sees all of my thoughts.

The Lord sees all of my feelings and keeps the watch on my heart.

Only the Lord can keep a watch on my heart.

Only the Lord can keep a watch on your heart.

Only the Lord always knows the real me.

Only the Lord always knows the real you.

I don't always know the real me.

You don't always know the real you.

I can't always keep a watch on my heart, because I don't always know my own heart.

You can't always keep a watch on your heart, because you don't always know your our own heart.

Only the Lord always knows what I will say before I say it.

Only the Lord always knows what I will do before I do it.

Only the Lord always knows what I think before I think it.

Only the Lord can always keep a watch on my heart.

I can mean you good and well.

You can mean me good and well.

If I am under a lot of stress, I can say something wrong in the spur of the moment.

I can do something wrong in the spur of the moment, which shows that I can't always keep a watch on my heart.

If you are under a lot of stress, you can say something wrong in spur-of-the-moment.

If you are under a lot of stress, you can do something wrong in the spur-of-the-moment, which shows that you can't always keep a watch on your heart.

I don't know what is ahead of me, and I can walk into something that can affect me in a good way or a bad way.

You don't know what is ahead of you, and you can walk into something that could cause you to react in a good way or in a bad way, which shows that you can't always keep a watch on your heart.

I can even go into the household of Faith and mean everyone good and well, but someone may rub me the wrong way and I can get defensive in my heart.

You can go into the household of faith and mean everyone good and well, but someone may say or do something that you don't like that you don't see coming and you may want to tell them off in anger.

I can't always keep a watch on my heart, because I don't always know my own heart.

You can't always keep a watch on your heart, because you don't always know your own heart.

Only the Lord Jesus Christ can always keep a watch on your heart and on my heart every day.

I don't know what I will say throughout the day.

I don't know everything that I will do throughout the day.

The Lord always knows every word that comes from my heart.

The Lord always knows everything I do that comes from my heart.

Only the Lord can always keep a watch on your heart and judge your heart.

I can't judge your heart, and you can't judge my heart.

I can say something and I won't know why I said it.

I can do something and I won't know why I did it.

You can say something and not know why you said it.

You can do something and not know why you did it.

The heart can be very complex, which goes to show that even some hereditary things in me and you can have an effect on our choices from the heart.

I can say some words that I'm not aware of that can have a good effect or a bad effect on someone else.

I can do something that I am not fully aware of that can have a good effect or a bad effect on someone else.

I can say something wrong and do something wrong, but that doesn't always define the meaning of my heart.

You can say something wrong and do something wrong, but that doesn't always define the true meaning of your heart.

You and I can never fool God by what we say and do.

The heart can never fool God, when the heart can sometimes not be transparent and control you and me so that we believe something is true when it is not.

Only the Lord can always keep a watch on our hearts.

You and I can fall asleep spiritually on our own hearts, and can believe that we always know our own hearts.

No Matter How

No matter how good you are, someone else may be more good than you.

No matter how nice you are, someone else may be nicer than you.

No matter how beautiful you look, someone else may be more beautiful than you.

No matter how strong you are, someone else may be stronger than you.

No matter how heroic you are, someone else may be more heroic than you.

No matter how happy you are, someone else may be more happier than than you.

No matter how sad you are, someone else may be sadder than you.

No matter how pretty you are, someone else may be prettier than you.

No matter how much you write, someone else may write more than you.

No matter how much you read, someone else may read more than you.

No matter how safe you are, someone else may be safer than you.

No matter how much you talk, someone else may talk more than you.

No matter how much you listen, someone else may listen more than you.

No matter how shy you are, someone else may be more shy than you.

No matter how bold you are, someone else may be bolder than you.

No matter how proud you are, someone else may be prouder than you.

No matter how brave you are, someone else may be braver than you.

No matter how charming you are, someone else may be more charming than you.

No matter how quiet you are, someone else may be quieter than you.

No matter how loud you are, someone else may be louder than you.

No matter how bad you are, someone may be worse than you.

No matter how genius you are, someone else may be more genius than you.

No matter how brilliant you are, someone else may be more brilliant than you.

No matter how intelligent you are, someone else may be more intelligent than you.

No matter how smart you are, someone else may be smarter than you.

No matter how tall you are, someone else may be taller than you.

No matter how short you are, someone else may be shorter than you.

No matter how big you are, someone else may be bigger than you.

No matter how small you are, someone else may be smaller than you.

No matter how holy you are, someone else may be holier than you.

No matter how righteous you are, someone else may be more righteous than you.

No matter how much you preach, someone else may be preaching more than you.

No matter how much Faith you have in Jesus Christ, someone else may have more faith in Jesus Christ.

No matter how much you love Jesus, someone else may love Jesus more than you.

No matter how much you obey Jesus, someone else may obey Jesus more than you.

No matter how much you work for Jesus, someone else may do more work for Jesus than you.

No matter how talented you are, someone else may be more talented than you.

No matter how gifted you are, someone else may be more gifted than you.

No matter how skillful you are, someone else may be more skillful than you.

No matter how hard you work, someone else may work harder than you.

No matter how many mistakes you make, someone else may make more mistakes than you.

No matter how many flaws you have, someone else may have more flaws than you.

No matter how many times you've failed, someone else may have failed more than you.

No matter how many times you win, someone else may have won more than you.

No matter how many times you lose, someone else may have lost more than you.

No matter how rich you are, someone else may be richer than you.

No matter how poor you are, someone else may be poorer than you.

No matter how many pets you have, someone else may have more pets than you.

No matter how sick you are, someone else may be sicker than you.

No matter how tough you are, someone else may be tougher than you.

No matter how wise you are, someone else may be wiser than you.

No matter how foolish you are, someone may be more foolish than you.

No matter how much you pray to Jesus, someone else may pray to Jesus more than you.

No matter how much you study the Bible, someone else may study the Bible more than you.

No matter how much you know the Bible scriptures, someone else may know the Bible scriptures better than you.

No matter how close you are to Jesus, someone else may be closer to Jesus than you.

No matter how much you have sinned, someone else may have sinned against the Lord more than you.

No matter how much favor you have with Jesus, someone else may have more favor with Jesus than you.

No matter how much you believe in Jesus, someone else may have more belief in Jesus than you.

No matter how much you reject Jesus, someone else may reject Jesus more than you.

No matter how honest you are, someone else may be more honest than you.

No matter how many lies you tell, someone else may tell more lies than you.

No matter how afraid you are, someone else may be more afraid than you.

No matter how loyal you are, someone else may be more loyal than you.

No matter how peaceful you are, someone else may be more peaceful than you.

No matter how manipulating you are, someone else may be more manipulating than you.

No matter how tactful you are, someone else may be more tactful than you.

No matter how careful you are, someone else may be more careful than you.

No matter how deceiving you are, someone else may be more deceiving than you.

No matter how prejudiced you are, someone else may be more prejudiced than you.

No matter how hateful you are, someone else may be more hateful than you.

No matter how evil you are, someone else may be more evil than you.

No matter how educated you are, someone else may be more educated than you.

No matter how much you are blessed by the Lord, someone else may be more blessed by the Lord than you.

No matter how much you put your trust in the Lord, someone else may put more trust in the Lord than you.

No matter how much time you spend with Jesus, our Lord, someone else may spend more time with Jesus than you.

No matter what you do in Jesus' name, someone else may do more good things in Jesus' holy name than you.

Who is Forevermore

You are not too genius for the Lord, who is forevermore genius than you.

You are not too brilliant for the Lord, who is forevermore brilliant than you.

You are not too intelligent for the Lord, who is forevermore intelligent than you.

You are not too smart for Lord, who is forevermore smarter than you.

You are not too proud for the Lord, who can do all things forever better than you.

You are not too wise for the Lord, whose foolishness is forever wiser than you.

You are not too good for the Lord, who is forevermore good than you.

You are not too faithful for the Lord, who is forevermore faithful than you.

You are not too trustworthy for the Lord, who is forevermore trustworthy than you.

You are not too true for the Lord, who is forevermore true than you.

You are not too transparent for the Lord, who is forevermore transparent than you.

You are not too real for the Lord, who is forevermore real than you.

You are not too temperate for the Lord, who is forevermore temperate than you.

You are not too holy for the Lord, who is forevermore holy than you.

You are not too righteous for the Lord, who is forevermore righteous than you.

You are not too strong for the Lord, who is forevermore stronger than you.

You are not too spiritual for the Lord, who is forevermore spiritual than you.

You are not too compassionate for the Lord, who is forevermore compassionate than you.

You are not too wealthy for the Lord, who is forevermore wealthy than you.

You are not too beautiful for the Lord, who is forevermore beautiful than you.

You are not too loving for the Lord, who is forevermore loving than you.

You are not too big for the Lord, who is forevermore bigger than you.

You are not too careful for the Lord, who is forevermore careful than you.

You are not too tactful for the Lord, who is forevermore tactful than you.

You are not too clever for the Lord, who is forevermore clever than you.

You are not too healthy for the Lord, who is forevermore healthy than you.

You are not too talkative for the Lord, who is forevermore talkative than you.

You are not too vibrant for the Lord, who is forevermore vibrant than you.

You are not too old for the Lord, who is forevermore the Ancient of Days.

You are not too free for the Lord, who is forevermore free than you.

You don't know too much for the Lord, He knows forever more things than you.

You can't see anything too much for the Lord, who sees everything and everyone forevermore than you.

You can't hear too much for the Lord, who hears everything and everyone forevermore than you.

You can't stay awake too much for the Lord, who is forevermore awake than you.

You can't be more joyful than the Lord, who is forevermore joyful than you.

You can't go to more places than the Lord, who is everywhere to go forevermore places than you.

You can't be more certain than the Lord, who is forevermore certain than you.

You can't be more on time than the Lord, who is forevermore on time than you.

You can't be more friendly than the Lord, who is forevermore friendly than you.

You can't be more brave than the Lord, who forevermore more brave than you.

You can't be more educated than the Lord, who is forevermore educated than you.

You can't be more superior the Lord, who is forevermore superior than you.

You can't be more secure than the Lord, who is forevermore secure than you.

You can't be more humble than the Lord, who is forevermore humble than you.

You can't be more skillful than the Lord, who is forevermore skillful than you.

Under the Sun

Under the sun, we move around here and there and usually ask no questions about where we should go.

Under the sun, many people write books and get them published but there is only one book of life that is published by God beyond the sun.

Under the sun, we have motives and intentions that will sooner or later reveal the real you and me.

Under the sun, all great people are not good people.

Under the sun, religion can twist and turn many people's minds until they think nothing about God.

Under the sun, many people make up their own religion that is far from being in line with God's holy word.

Under the sun, we will make some mistakes.

Under the sun, we will learn some things the easy way and we will learn some things the hard way.

Under the sun, many people will wash the dirt off of their hands and believe that they haven't done anything wrong.

Under the sun, many people will do evil and believe that it is good.

Under the sun, we are all alike when it comes to being a human being.

Under the sun, we are all alike when it comes to being alive.

Under the sun, we are all alike when it comes to dying.

Under the sun, we all have a sinful nature.

Under the sun, we all need to love and obey Jesus Christ.

Under the sun, we all can be saved in Jesus Christ.

Under the sun, we all fall short of the glory of God.

Under the sun, we all have sins to confess and repent of unto the Lord Jesus Christ.

Under the sun, we all can eat the spiritual food of God's holy word that will never dull our senses.

Under the sun, we all have one thing in common and that is God created us all in His image.

Under the sun, we all are people living here on earth together every day.

Under the sun, we all have a destiny that can't pass by God.

Under the sun, we all have a destiny that God knows about.

Under the sun, we all have a destiny that God will judge.

Under the sun, many people will pass by you and me every day, but no one can pass by God who is everywhere in heaven and everywhere under the sun.

There are many people who you and I will cross paths with only once under the sun.

There are many people who will drive past you and me on the highway and local roads, but no one can drive past God who is everywhere in heaven and everywhere under the sun.

There are many people who will walk past you and me in the stores and in the shopping malls, but no one can walk past God who is everywhere in heaven and everywhere under the sun.

Under the sun, we are born into this world and we will one day die in this world, but God lives forever in heaven and lives forever under the sun.

Under the sun, many people believe that there is no God, but many other people believe that there is a God who is with us under the sun.

Under the sun, we all don't know the day that we will die, but while we live we can choose to live unto Jesus Christ who can save us from our sins under the sun.

Under the sun, we all have free will choice given to us by God.

No one can overpower you and me and make us not choose doing right instead of wrong under the sun.

Under the sun, we all must eat food and drink water to live day after day.

Under the sun, we all must breathe air in and out of our nostrils to live day after day.

Under the sun, we all must take a bath or take a shower to keep our bodies clean.

Under the sun, we all must brush our teeth to keep our breath fresh.

Under the sun, we all will have some kind of influence on one another.

Under the sun, we all have some flaws.

Under the sun, we all need to be loved.

Under the sun, none of us wants to be lied to.

Under the sun, we all want to be accepted.

Under the sun, we all want to be loved and not be hated.

Under the sun, we all are human and feel some pain.

We can say this and say that under the sun, but God's word will never change.

We can do this and do that under the sun, but God will keep His oath to us under the sun.

Under the sun, we all have a limit, but many people will go over their limit and shorten their own lives under the sun.

Under the sun, we all have a purpose for being here in this world and everybody has a good purpose given to them by God.

Under the sun, we all can choose to fulfill our purpose, which is to love and obey Jesus Christ.

The Moonlight Glow of Time

The moonlight glow of time is the time that it takes to mature, and that won't happen overnight under the moonlight's glow.

The moonlight glow of time is the time that it takes to get experience, and that won't happen overnight under the moonlight's glow.

The moonlight glow of time is the time it takes to grow up, and that won't happen overnight under the moonlight's glow.

The moonlight glow of time is the time it takes to write a book, and that won't happen overnight under the moonlight's glow.

The moonlight glow of time is the time it takes to get to know people, and that won't happen overnight under the moonlight's glow.

The moonlight glow of time is the time it takes for emotional and physical wounds to heal, and that won't happen overnight under the moonlight's glow.

The moonlight glow of time is the time it takes to improve in life, and that won't happen overnight under the moonlight's glow.

The moonlight glow of time is the time it takes to learn new things in life, and that won't happen overnight under the moonlight's glow.

The moonlight glow of time is the time it takes to get old, and that won't happen overnight under the moonlight's glow.

The moonlight glow of time is the time it takes for a baby to be born, and that won't happen overnight under the moonlight's glow.

The moonlight glow of time is the time it takes to get an education, and that won't happen overnight under the moonlight's glow.

Moonlight glow time of is the time it takes to make a good name for yourself, and that won't happen overnight under the moonlight's glow.

The moonlight glow of time is the time it takes to spiritually mature in the Lord, and that won't happen overnight under the moonlight's glow.

The moonlight glow of time is the time it takes to grow strong in the Lord, and that won't happen overnight under the moonlight's glow.

The moonlight glow of time is the time it takes to obey the Lord, and that won't happen overnight under the moonlight's glow.

The moonlight glow of time is the time it takes to be spiritually cleansed in the Lord, and that won't happen overnight under the moonlight's glow.

The moonlight glow of time is the time it takes to win souls to love and obey the Lord, and that won't happen overnight under the moonlight's glow.

The moonlight glow of time is the time it takes for dreams to come true, and that won't happen overnight under the moonlight's glow.

The moonlight glow of time is the time it takes to learn from our mistakes, and that won't happen overnight under the moonlight's glow.

The moonlight glow of time is the time it takes for many people to forgive those who hurt them, and that won't happen overnight under the moonlight's glow.

The moonlight glow of time is the time it takes for many people to realize that the truth will set them free from life, and that won't happen overnight under the moonlight's glow.

The moonlight glow time is the time it takes for many people to repent and turn to Jesus, and that won't happen overnight under the moonlight's glow.

The moonlight glow of time is the time it takes for many people to wise up and do what is right, and that won't happen overnight under the moonlight's glow.

The moonlight glow of time is the time it takes for many church folks to love one another, and that won't happen overnight under the moonlight's glow.

The moonlight glow of time is the time it takes for many church folks to come to one accord, and that won't happened overnight under the moonlight's glow.

The moonlight glow of time is the time it takes for many church folks to truly have faith in the Lord, and that won't happen overnight under the moonlight's glow.

The moonlight glow of time is the time it takes for many church folks to humble themselves unto the Lord, and that won't happen overnight under the moonlight's glow.

The moonlight glow of time is the time it takes for we church folks to be more and more like Jesus, and that won't happen overnight under the moonlight's glow.

The moonlight glow of time is the time it took for me to repent and to sincerely turn to the Lord Jesus Christ, and that didn't happen overnight under the moonlight's glow.

A Lot of People

A lot of people don't believe in Jesus Christ.

A lot of people don't want to believe in Jesus Christ.

A lot of people don't want to have anything to do with Jesus.

A lot of people won't speak the name of Jesus.

A lot of people don't want to speak the name of Jesus.

A lot of people don't want to hear the name of Jesus.

A lot of people don't want to hear anything about Jesus.

A lot of people reject Jesus every day.

A lot of people don't love Jesus Christ.

A lot of people won't read any books about Jesus Christ.

A lot of people won't listen to any sermons about Jesus Christ.

A lot of people don't want any Bible studies about Jesus Christ.

A lot of people don't want to read any poems about Jesus Christ.

A lot of people talk bad about Jesus Christ.

A lot of people believe that they are more holy than Jesus Christ.

A lot of people believe that they are more righteous than Jesus Christ.

A lot of people believe that they are more powerful than Jesus Christ.

A lot of people believe that they are richer than Jesus Christ.

A lot of people believe that they are more spiritual than Jesus Christ.

A lot of people believe that they are smarter than Jesus Christ.

Lucifer believed that he was better than Jesus Christ.

Lucifer believed that he was more righteous than Jesus Christ.

Lucifer believed that he was holier than Jesus Christ.

The Pharisees believed they were holier than Jesus Christ.

The Pharisees believed that they were more righteous than Jesus Christ.

The Pharisees believed that they were more powerful than Jesus Christ.

The Pharisees believed that they were smarter than Jesus Christ.

The Pharisees believe that they were more spiritual than Jesus Christ.

A lot of people hate Jesus Christ.

A lot of people mock Jesus Christ.

A lot of people will lie about Jesus Christ.

The Pharisees lied about Jesus Christ.

A lot of people hate you and me for believing in Jesus Christ.

A lot of people will lie about you and me because we love and obey Jesus Christ.

A lot of people will not be saved in Jesus Christ.

A lot of people despise Jesus Christ.

A lot of people despise you and me for believing in Jesus Christ.

A lot of people despise you and me for working for Jesus Christ.

A lot of people have turned their backs on Jesus Christ.

A lot of people have turned their backs on you and me for believing in Jesus Christ.

A lot of people will not confess their sins to Jesus Christ.

A lot of people will not repent of their sins to Jesus Christ.

A lot of people don't believe that Jesus Christ is the Son of God.

A lot of people don't believe that Jesus Christ can save them from their sins.

A lot of people don't believe that Jesus Christ can cleanse them of their sins.

A lot of people don't believe that Jesus Christ is coming back again.

A lot of people don't believe that Jesus Christ is the way, truth, and life.

A lot of people don't believe that Jesus Christ created all things.

A lot of people don't believe that Jesus Christ is one with God.

A lot of people don't believe that Jesus Christ can heal them.

A lot of people don't want to believe that Jesus Christ can heal them.

A lot of people don't believe that Jesus Christ can help them.

A lot of people don't believe that Jesus Christ will never leave them or forsake them.

A lot of people don't believe that Jesus Christ is real.

A lot of people don't believe that Jesus Christ can protect them.

A lot of people don't believe that Jesus Christ is always ahead of them.

A lot of people don't believe that Jesus Christ can make a way out of no way.

A lot of people don't believe that Jesus Christ can give them the victory.

A lot of people don't believe that Jesus Christ loves them.

A lot of people don't believe that Jesus Christ knows all of their motives.

A lot of people don't believe that Jesus Christ knows all of their intentions.

A lot of people don't believe that Jesus Christ knows all of their thoughts.

A lot of people don't believe that Jesus Christ knows all of their feelings.

A lot of people don't believe that Jesus Christ knows all of their hearts.

A lot of people don't believe that Jesus Christ knows all of their minds .

A lot of people don't believe that Jesus Christ is the King of Kings.

A lot of people don't believe that Jesus Christ is the Lord of Lords.

A lot of people don't believe that Jesus Christ existed before all things.

A lot of people don't believe that Jesus Christ was a sinless man.

The Pharisees didn't believe that Jesus Christ was a sinless man.

A lot of people don't believe that Jesus Christ brought them this far in their lives.

A lot of people don't believe that it's Jesus Christ who gives them a second chance.

A lot of people don't believe that it is Jesus Christ who lets them live to see another day, week, month, and year.

A lot of people don't believe that it is Jesus Christ who lets them live to be old and have gray hair.

A lot of people don't call on the name of Jesus Christ.

A lot of people don't want to call on the name of Jesus Christ.

A lot of people don't give any praise to Jesus Christ.

A lot of people don't want to give praise to Jesus Christ.

A lot of people don't give any glory to Jesus Christ.

A lot of people don't want to give any glory to Jesus Christ.

A lot of people don't talk about Jesus Christ.

A lot of people don't want to talk about Jesus Christ.

A lot of people don't listen to any songs about Jesus Christ.

A lot of people don't want to listen to any songs about Jesus Christ.

A lot of people don't sing any songs about Jesus Christ.

A lot of people don't want to sing any songs about Jesus Christ.

A lot of people don't put their hope in Jesus Christ.

A lot of people don't want to put their hope in Jesus Christ.

A lot of people won't give their hearts to Jesus Christ.

A lot of people don't want to give their hearts to Jesus Christ.

A lot of people don't put their trust in Jesus Christ.

A lot of people don't want to put their trust in Jesus Christ.

A lot of people will die being lost in their sins for not being saved in Jesus Christ.

A lot of people don't care if they die being lost in their sins.

A lot of people don't believe that it's Jesus Christ who gives them strength.

A lot of people don't believe that it's Jesus Christ who gives them wisdom.

A lot of people don't believe that it's Jesus Christ who lets them get educated.

A lot of people don't believe that it's Jesus Christ who gives them talents.

A lot of people don't believe that it is Jesus Christ who gives them the ability to be skillful.

A lot of people don't believe that it's Jesus Christ who gives them the ability to be successful.

A lot of people don't believe that it's Jesus Christ who allows them to get rich.

A lot of people don't believe that it's Jesus Christ who gives them the ability to get knowledge.

A lot of people don't believe that it's Jesus Christ who gives them good health.

A lot of people don't believe that it's Jesus Christ who gives things to us and can take them back.

A lot of people don't believe that it is Jesus Christ who allowed them to be who they are today.

A lot of people don't believe that Jesus Christ can change their lives.

A lot of people don't believe that Jesus Christ can make their lives better.

A lot of people don't believe that Jesus Christ can save the worst sinner.

A lot of people don't believe that they will have to face Jesus Christ to determine their destinies.

No one's destiny can go beyond Jesus Christ.

You Can Only Live Your Life

You can only live your life the way that you want to live.

You can only live your life in a way that will have a good or a bad effect on others.

You can only live your life in peace or in conflict.

You can only live your life loving yourself or not loving yourself.

You can only live your life being in control of yourself or not being in control of yourself.

You can onlt live your life one day at a time.

You can only live your life in fear or in boldness.

You can only live your life, no matter what someone else may think.

You can only live your life, no matter what someone else may say.

You can only live your life, no matter what someone else might do.

You can only live your life, no matter what someone else dreams.

You can only live your life, no matter how someone else feels.

You can only live your life being truthful or living a lie.

You can only live your life that God will hold you accountable for.

You can only live your life loving Jesus or not loving Jesus Christ.

You can only live your life loving your neighbor or not loving your neighbors.

You can only live your life under all the stars.

You can only live your life because no one else can live it for you.

You can only live your life by your own free will choices.

You can only live your life to be a blessing to others or to be a curse to others.

You can only live your life being faithful unto the Lord or not being faithful unto the Lord.

You can only live your life being obedient unto the Lord or not being obedient unto the Lord.

You can only live your life putting your trust in the Lord or not putting your trust in the Lord.

You can only live your life being saved in the Lord or not being saved in the Lord.

You can only live your life doing right or doing wrong.

You can only live your life being content or not being content.

You can only live your life and God will be your only judge.

You can only live your life to destine you to go to heaven or hell.

You can only live your life that God gave you to live.

I Want to Help People Make it to Heaven

I want to help people make it to heaven with my inspirational poetry that I love to write about my Lord and Savior Jesus Christ.

I want people to read my poems and know that they are written for them to learn about Jesus.

I want to help people make it to Heaven because that's where I want to go one day to be with Jesus forever.

I want to help people make it to heaven by showing them the life that I love to live unto my Lord Jesus Christ every day.

I want to help people make it to heaven with the knowledge of God's holy word that I love to share with everyone.

I want to help people make it to heaven with my testimony that I love to share with them so that they can know Jesus brought me this far in my life.

I want to help people make it to heaven because only Jesus Christ has a heaven to put people in.

I want to help people make it to heaven because from the beginning of this world Jesus created mankind and womankind to live with Him in heaven and on earth without sin.

I want to help people make it to heaven, even though, in the end, not everyone will make it there.

I want to help people make it to heaven, even though there are many people who don't want to hear anything about Jesus Christ.

I want to help people make it to heaven, even though there are people who believe that I am wasting my time for believing in Jesus Christ.

I want to help people make it to heaven, even though there are people in the church who will not be blessed by my spiritual gifts from the Lord.

I want to help people make it to heaven, because I love Jesus and Jesus will come back again one day.

I want to help people make it to heaven with the truth of God's holy word.

I want to help people make it to heaven with the fruit of the spirit living in me that represents my Lord and Savior Jesus Christ.

I want to help people make it to heaven by showing them my faith in Jesus Christ, which no one can judge.

I want to help people make it to heaven, even though there are people in the church who will accuse me of not being a Christian.

I want to help people make it to heaven, even though there are people who don't want to deny themselves, pick up their crosses and follow Jesus Christ.

I want to help people make it to heaven, even though there are people who believe that they are self-made and don't need Jesus, who gives them life, health, and strength to prosper in life.

A Spiritual Birthday

The day, month, and year that we were born is our physical birthday that comes around once a year.

Everybody should be glad to see another birthday because that lets us know it is a blessing from the Lord to get another year older.

Many people don't like to tell people how old they are, like it's a wrong thing to tell their age.

A lot of people who are up in age don't truly appreciate another birthday because they see wrinkles and moles on their bodies, but they should see another birthday as a miracle — especially when compared to the dead, who can't have any more birthdays.

Living to see another birthday is greater than all the money in this world, which we can't spend if we are dead.

If we are dead, we can't even spend one penny.

No one should ever feel ashamed about their age, because advancing age lets us know that we are still alive in the land of the living.

Aging is always a blessing from the Lord.

Having another birthday is a miracle that we especially see in this world where many wicked people live a dangerous life and don't live to see another birthday.

Many foolish people should have died in their risk-taking behaviors, but they live to see another birthday.

Our birthday is only once a year, but many people don't live to see another year.

Our birthday is a day of great remembrance for you and me, even if no one else remembers our birthdays.

There is a spiritual birthday that we have every day, every month, and every year.

Being born in our new spiritual birth will never age us and we will never grow old spiritually.

We will get no wrinkles or moles in our spiritual birth.

Being born again in Jesus Christ will keep us young in our minds and hearts every day, every month, and every year.

No one will ever have to feel ashamed about telling their spiritual age to anyone.

You will know the day that you and I were baptized in the Lord is a good thing.

If we can be happy to see another birthday that will show us getting older, then we can be even happier to have a spiritual birthday that will never age us or causes us to walk with a bent back,.

We will walk spiritually upright and vibrant in the Lord every day, every month, and every year.

Don't Judge People

Don't judge people if they don't believe what you believe.

Don't judge people if they don't believe the truth that you believe.

Don't judge people if they don't know the truth that you know.

Don't judge people if they don't live the truth that you live.

Don't judge people if they are not spiritual like you.

Don't judge people if they are not strong in the Lord like you.

Don't judge people if they don't know what you know.

Don't judge people if they don't do what you do.

Don't judge people if they are different from you.

Don't judge people if they don't say what you want them to say.

Don't judge people if they don't do what you want them to do.

Don't judge people if they disagree with you.

Don't judge people if they don't love you.

Don't judge people if they don't see eye-to-eye with you.

Don't judge people if they don't talk to you.

It's never a good thing to judge people.

You and I don't know what is deep down in someone's heart.

You and I don't truly know our own hearts.

How can you and I truly know people's hearts when we don't know what is in our own hearts?

You and I can't judge people's hearts.

Only God always knows everyone's heart and can judge everyone's heart.

I can't judge you and you can't judge me.

Only God can judge you and only God can judge me.

Only God knows all of our strengths and all of our weaknesses.

Only God knows all that we can ever do.

Only God knows all that we can ever bear.

Only God always knows what we will say before we say it.

Only God knows all of our motives.

God is the only judge to judge everyone's past.

Don't judge people if they don't believe in God's son, Jesus Christ.

The Lord Amazes Me

When I graduated from high school, I joined the Army to serve my country.

I was young and excited about being in the military with my friends from my hometown.

When I was in the Army, I was a combat engineer being prepared to fight in a war.

I made the mistake of using illegal drugs and that caused me to have a nervous breakdown.

At that time, I lost a lot of my memory, including pretty much everything that I had learned in school, as well as what I had learned in the military.

I was hospitalized and was discharged from the Army with a medical honorable discharge.

For years and years, my memory was not good at all.

Even up to this day, the Lord amazes me with the memory I do have.

The Lord amazes me with the talent to write poetry about Him, even though I don't remember a lot of the poetry I write.

The Lord amazes me with so many poems that He gives to me to write about Him.

The Lord has blessed me to get books of poetry published, along with many of my poems being produced into gospel songs.

The Lord amazes me with a mind to think about Him every day.

My memory is mostly about doing the Lord's holy will.

The Lord amazes me with a mind to remember some things that I need to know to survive in this world.

Some things that I learned in school have come back to me.

Some things that I learned in the Army have come back to me.

The Lord amazes me with a mind to remember my kinfolks and some friends that I have.

It's a miracle to me that my memory is as good as it is today.

I know that my memory is as good as it is because of my Lord and Savior Jesus Christ, who has blessed me with good doctors to give me good medicine to help me stay well in my mind so that I can remember what I need to remember to survive in this world.

I will read my Bible and not remember a lot of what I read.

I've thought many times how it would be so great if I could remember a lot of what I read.

The Lord amazes me by giving me His holy spirit to bring back my memory of what I read in the Bible so I can share it with others.

The Lord amazes me with how far He has brought me.

It amazes me that I can remember anything, especially well enough to write it down in many poems about my Lord, who I don't want to ever forget.

Many People Know Better

Many people know better and love everybody.

A tsunami doesn't know better and will flood, sweep people's houses away, and take their lives.

Many people know better and treat everybody right.

An earthquake doesn't know better and will shake, break down people's houses, and take their lives.

Many people know better and help those who they can help.

A tornado doesn't know better and will rip people's houses down and take their lives.

Many people know better and respect everybody.

A hurricane doesn't know better and will blow down people's houses and take their lives.

Many people know better and talk nice to everybody.

A wildfire doesn't know better and will burn down people's houses and take their lives.

Many people know better and give a kind eye look to everyone.

A snow blizzard doesn't know better and will freeze people and take their lives.

Many people know better and are good to everybody.

A heatwave doesn't know better and will give people heat stroke and take their lives.

Many people know better and are fair to everybody.

A landslide doesn't know better and will take people's houses off their foundations and take people's lives.

Many people know better and give encouragement to everybody.

A sinkhole doesn't know better and will sink people's houses down into its hole and take their lives.

For the people who know better, doing what is right is what they do; but those who do not know better can be like natural disasters.

When the people who don't know better don't do what is right, God will wink his eye at their ignorance, but will not excuse their sins.

But, the people who do know better and don't do right are worse off than the people who don't know better and don't do right.

I Can Always

I can always talk to You early in the morning, O Lord, when I can't talk to anyone else.

I can always talk to You late at night, O Lord, when I can't talk to anyone else.

I can always put my trust in You, O Lord, when I can't trust anyone else to always be there for me.

I can always believe in You, O Lord, when I can't believe in anyone else because they have sins to confess and repent of.

I can always love You, O Lord, when I can't always love myself, who doesn't know what love is if I don't love You with all of my heart, soul, and strength.

I can always follow You, O Lord, when I can't follow this world that is temporary below You, O Lord, who is eternal.

I can always keep my eyes on You, O Lord, when I can't keep my eyes on people who are not perfect and will say something wrong or do something wrong.

I can always get strength in You, O Lord, who knows my every weakness and will mold me and shape me into being more and more like You.

I can always obey You, O Lord, when I can't always obey people who can make mistakes.

I can always be like You, O Lord, when I can't always be like people who can change on me.

You, O Lord, will never change on me.

I can always have hope in You, O Lord, when I can't always have hope in people who can let me down.

I can always have faith in You, O Lord, who will never fail me because You always know what is best for me.

You save me from my sins, even if You have to shorten my life to save me from being lost.

I can always keep my will in Your holy will, O Lord, because if I do my own will, I will break Your Commandments that are Your will for me to keep.

The More

The more strong we are in the Lord, the more the devil will attack us with his sins.

The more that we know about God's holy word, the more the Lord will hold us accountable for what we know is right and wrong to do.

The more close we are to the Lord, the more we must deny ourselves and pick up our crosses to follow Jesus.

The more we sin against the Lord, the more lost we are away from the Lord.

The more we pray to the Lord, the more the devil will stay away from us.

The more we humble ourselves unto the Lord, the more pride will leave us alone.

The more we love the Lord, the more we will obey the Lord.

The more we go through trials for our Lord Jesus Christ's name sake, the more we will be like Him.

The more we love one another, the more we are in unity with one another.

The more we wait on the Lord, the more content we will be.

The more we trust the Lord, the more we don't trust this world.

The more we work for the Lord, the more joyful we are in the Lord.

The more that we forgive others, the more healthy we are in our minds, hearts, and bodies.

The more we give to the Lord, the more secure we will feel in the Lord.

The more we please the Lord, the more the Lord will bless us.

All Around The World

O Lord, you are so good all around the world where You love everybody all the same.

Your goodness, O Lord, brings tears to my eyes.

I see Your love everywhere, even for all of the animals that belong to You.

O Lord, You are so good all around the world, where You want to save everybody from being lost in their sins.

All around the world Your goodness, O Lord, leads people to repent of their sins.

All around the world, Your goodness, O Lord, makes life on earth still exist today.

O Lord, you are so good all around the world, where Your presence is real in life.

Your goodness, O Lord, makes good things happen in people's lives all around the world.

Your goodness, O Lord, makes the sun rise and the sun set.

Your goodness, O Lord, makes the moon glow all night long.

Your goodness, O Lord, makes the stars sparkle all night long.

Your goodness, O Lord, holds this whole world together every day and every night.

O Lord, you are so good all around the world, where You keep nations from destroying this world.

O Lord, you are so good all around the world, where all little children belong to You.

All around the world, O Lord, You provide the air for everybody to breathe in and out of their nostrils.

O Lord, You are so good all around the world, where you give everybody the free will choice to choose life or death.

O Lord, You are so good all around the world, where You give everybody the dry land to live on.

Your goodness, O Lord, reaches from the north and south and east and west side of this world.

All around the world, there are many people who know that You are so good to them, O Lord.

O Lord, you are so good all around the world, where everybody will not be good to one another.

O Lord, you are so good all around the world, where everybody will not be good to You, O Lord.

O Lord, you are so good all around the world, where everybody will not acknowledge that You are so good, O Lord.

O Lord, you are so good all around the world, where many people will mistake Your goodness for luck.

All around the world, Your goodness, O Lord, is miraculous and keeps death from taking away everybody's breath.

There Are People Who Believe

There are people who believe that they are better than you if they look better than you.

There are people who believe that they are better than you if they are taller than you.

There are people who believe that they are better than you if they are bigger than you.

There are people who believe that they are better than you if they are stronger than you.

There are people who believe that they are better than you if they are smarter than you.

There are people who believe that they are better than you if they are more educated than you.

There are people who believe that they are better than you if they are more talented than you.

There are people who believe that they are better than you if they are more skillful than you.

There are people who believe that they are better than you if they are living in a bigger house than you.

There are people who believe that they are better than you if they have more vehicles than you.

There are people who believe that they are better than you if they can do what you can't do.

There are people who believe that they are better than you if they have more money than you.

There people who believe that they are better than you if they know the Bible scriptures more than you do.

There people who believe that they are better than you if they go to church more than you do.

There are people who believe that they are better than you if their skin complexion is lighter than your skin complexion.

There are people who believe that they are better than you if their health is better than your health.

There are people who believe that they are better than you if they have achieved what you have not achieved.

Only Jesus Christ is worthy to be better than you and me because He is the Son of God.

Only Jesus Christ is worthy to be better than you and me because He had no sins when He lived here on earth.

Only Jesus Christ is worthy to be better than you and me because He gave up his life on the cross and became sin to save us from our sins.

There are people who believe that they are better than God; they are like the devil because he also believes that he is better than God.

Holy Word, O Lord

Your holy word, O Lord, helps me to be aware of Your will for me.

Your holy word, O Lord, helps me to be aware of the choices that I make.

Your holy word, O Lord, helps me to be aware of the truth.

Your holy word, O Lord, helps me to be aware of the devil's lies.

Your holy word, O Lord, helps me to be aware of what is right.

Your holy word, O Lord, helps me to be aware of what is wrong.

Your holy word, O Lord, helps me to be aware of what is good.

Your only word, O Lord, helps me to be aware of what is evil.

Your holy word, O Lord, helps me to be aware of the devil's temptations.

Your holy word, O Lord, helps me to be aware of what is going on around me.

Your holy word, O Lord, helps me to be aware of what is real.

Your holy word, O Lord, helps me to be aware of other people.

Your holy word, O Lord, helps me to be aware of myself.

Your holy word, O Lord, helps me to be aware of what is going on in this world.

Your holy word, O Lord, helps me to be aware of my conscience.

Your holy word, O Lord, helps me to be aware of what I say.

Your holy word, O Lord, helps me to be aware of what I do.

Your holy word, O Lord, helps me to be aware of what other people say.

Your holy word, O Lord, helps me to be aware of what other people do.

Your holy word, O Lord, helps me to be aware of my past life.

Your holy word, O Lord, helps me to be aware of my present life.

Your holy word, O Lord, keeps my eyes open to Your will for me and what You want me to do.

Your holy word, O Lord, is my eye-opener to all of the truth.

Your holy word, O Lord, is my eye-opener to life.

Your holy word, O Lord, is my eye-opener to the past.

Your holy word, O Lord, is my eye-opener to the present.

Your holy word, O Lord, is my eye-opener to the truth.

Your holy word, O Lord, is my eye-opener to life.

Your holy word, O Lord, is my eye-opener to the future.

Your holy word, O Lord, is my eye-opener to You.

Your holy word, O Lord, in my eye-opener to everything in this world.

Your holy word, O Lord, is my eye-opener to my life.

Your holy word, O Lord, is my eye-opener to freedom.

Your holy word, O Lord, is my eye-opener to my trials.

Your holy word, O Lord, tis my eye-opener to my destiny.

In Jesus' Hands

It's always good to put our problems in Jesus' hands and leave them there.

We need to put our bad dreams in Jesus' hands and leave them there.

If we put things in our own hands, they can slip out of our hands.

If we put things in our own hands, they can fall out of our hands.

We can always put our lives in Jesus' almighty hands because we are nothing without Him.

We can always put our dreams in Jesus' almighty hands that nothing can fall out of.

Jesus' hands can always hold our problems and make them go away.

Jesus' hands can always hold our bad dreams and make them fade away and not come true.

Jesus' hands can always hold our lives and let us live many years if it is in His will.

We always need to put our problems in Jesus' hands and leave them there.

Whatever we put in Jesus' hands, no one can take out of His hands.

Whatever we give to Jesus, He will not drop it from His hands.

Our problems won't drop out of His hands.

Our bad dreams won't drop out of His hands.

Our lives won't drop out of His hands.

Jesus' hands hold the universe in place.

Jesus' hands hold this world in its place.

Jesus' hands hold the heavens in their place.

Things can slip out of our hands.

Things can fall out of our hands.

Our hands can lose their grip.

Jesus' hands will never lose their grip on our problems.

Jesus' hands will never lose their grip on our dreams.

Jesus' hands will never lose their grip on our lives.

Jesus' hands are always strong and will fight against our enemies.

Jesus' hands are always strong and will pick us up if we fall down or get into trouble.

Jesus' hands are always strong and will grip our souls and save us from being lost in sin.

Jesus' hands are always strong and will carry all of our needs.

We can always put our dispair, sorrows, and disappointments in Jesus' hands.

Our past, present, and future are all in Jesus' hands.

Even death can't take us out of Jesus' hands, because He holds eternal life and gives it to you and me for being saved in Him.

In Jesus' hands are all the things that He created.

It doesn't matter if you and I refuse to put our problems in His hands, His hands will never lose their grip on eternity.

By the Choices We Make

We know who we are by the choices we make.

We know that we are wise by the choices we make.

We know that we are foolish by the choices we make.

We know that we are good by the choices we make.

We know that we are bad by the choices we make.

We know that we are Christians by the choices we make.

The choices we make show and tell who we are.

The choices we make can prolong our Lives.

The choices we make can shorten our lives.

We will reap what we sow by the choices we make.

We are aware of many choices that we make.

The choices that we are not aware of are still choices we make in an ignorant way.

We all make choices every day, even though we don't always choose our words to say.

We know that we are living right by the choices we make.

We regret things by the choices we make.

The choices we make can give us joy.

The choices we make can give us sorrow.

The choices we make can tell the truth about us.

The choices we make can cause us to be lost in our sins.

We can know our destiny by the choices we make.

We know that we are saved in Jesus Christ by the choices we make.

Many people are rich because of the choices they make.

Many people are poor because of the choices they make.

Many people are healthy because of the choices they make.

Many people are sick because of the choices they make.

Many people are still alive because of the choices they make.

Many people are dead because of the choices they made.

Loving and obeying the Lord Jesus Christ is the best choice we can make every day that we choose to love and obey the Lord Jesus Christ.

Living by Faith

Living by faith doesn't mean that we can do away with God's Commandments.

Faith and works go together because Jesus says, "If you love me you will keep my Commandments."

Faith without works is dead and works without faith is dead.

Living by faith doesn't mean that we can willfully sin against the Lord and it will be all right with Him.

God hates sin that breaks His laws.

If we believe in Jesus Christ, then we should believe that His laws are good for us to keep every day.

Living by faith doesn't mean that we can live our lives any kind of way we want.

Just because we are saved by grace doesn't mean that we have a right to break God's Commandments.

God's grace is His Son, Jesus Christ, who will save us from our sins if we confess and repent unto Him.

Living by faith is believing in Jesus Christ, who kept the Commandments of God when He lived on earth without sin.

If Jesus kept his Father's Commandments, then so can we because that shows our love for God.

Faith and keeping God's laws go together — we can't separate the two.

If children love their parents, they will obey their parents.

Obedience is proof of them loving their parents.

It's the same way with you and me obeying the Lord because we love Him.

Obeying the Lord and keeping his Commandments shows we love Him.

The only way to love God is to keep His Commandments.

Living by faith in Jesus Christ means that we will do what He says.

Living by faith in Jesus Christ means that our actions will be in line with God's holy word.

Living by faith in Jesus Christ means that we will live our lives to please Jesus by obeying His holy law.

Faith and keeping God's Commandments go together.

Children have faith in their parents to take care of them and to tell them the right things to do.

Jesus tells us the right things to do, and that is to keep His Commandments to show our love for Him.

Our faith in Him is loving Him and obeying Him.

The Pandemic of Sin

The pandemic of sin is worldwide every day and every night.

The pandemic of sin is the worst kind of pandemic every day and every night.

Murders are a pandemic of sin all around the world.

Theft is a pandemic of sin all around the world.

Fornication is a pandemic of sin all around the world.

Adultery is a pandemic of sin all around the world.

Lies are a pandemic of sin all around the world.

Deceptions are a pandemic of sin all around the world.

Prejudice is a pandemic of sin all around the world.

Injustice is a pandemic of sin all around the world.

Strife is a pandemic all around the world.

Greed is a pandemic of sin all around the world.

Hatred is a pandemic of sin all around the world.

Oppression is a pandemic of sin all around the world.

Manipulation is a pandemic of sin all around the world.

Discontentment is a pandemic of sin all around the world.

Pride is a pandemic of sin all around the world.

Homosexuality is a pandemic of sin all around the world.

Envy is a pandemic of sin all around the world.

Holding grudges is a pandemic of sin all around the world.

Jealousy is a pandemic of sin all around the world

Selfishness is a pandemic of sin all around the world.

Disobedience is a pandemic of sin all around the world.

Breaking God's holy law is a pandemic of sin all around the world.

Rejecting Jesus Christ is a pandemic of sin all around the world.

Rebellion against God is a pandemic of sin all around the world.

Turning one's back on Jesus Christ is a pandemic of sin all around the world.

Stand Up and Pick Up Your Mat

Stand up in Jesus' name and pick up your mat of doubt and walk, putting your trust in Jesus Christ.

Stand up in Jesus' name and pick up your mat of pride and walk in humility unto Jesus Christ.

Stand up in Jesus' name and pick up your mat of bias and walk in loving everyone who Jesus Christ loves.

Stand up in Jesus' name and pick up your mat of manipulation and walk in being fair and not wanting to be in control of people's lives, because that is something that Jesus Christ would not do.

Stand up in Jesus' name and pick up your mat of jealousy and walk in being happy for others who have accomplished some good things in their lives, especially in Jesus Christ's holy name.

Stand up in Jesus' name and pick up your mat of unforgiveness and walk in forgiving people for doing you wrong, because Jesus Christ will forgive you of your sins.

Stand up in Jesus' name and pick up your mat of fear and walk boldly, especially when spreading the gospel of Jesus Christ in your testimony, gospel songs, knowledge of God's holy word, and also in your living sermons.

Stand up in Jesus' name and pick up your mat of believing that your good works will save you as you walk in faith in Jesus Christ, who is the only one who can save you from your sins.

Stand up in Jesus' name and pick up your mat of disobedience and walk in obedience unto Jesus Christ by keeping His Commandments day after day.

Stand up in Jesus' name and pick up your mat of trying to out-reason Jesus Christ and walk in the truth of Jesus that will set you free from lies that can't reason with Jesus who is the truth.

Stand up in Jesus' name and pick up your mat of making excuses for your sins and instead walk in confessing and repenting of your sins to Jesus Christ, who is the only one you can turn to and be saved.

Fear Can Be a Good Thing

Fear can be a good thing for you and me when it makes us afraid to walk near a poisonous snake.

Fear can be a good thing for you and me when it makes us afraid to jump off of a high bridge.

Fear can be a good thing for you and me when it makes us afraid to drink polluted water.

Fear can be a good thing for you and me when it makes us afraid to eat rotten food.

Fear can be a good thing for you and me when it makes us afraid to walk in front of a speeding car.

Fear can be a good thing for you and me when it makes us afraid to fight in a war without being trained to fight.

Fear can be a good thing for you and me when it makes us afraid to preach a sermon when it is not our gift.

Fear can be a good thing for you and me when it makes us afraid to teach a bible school lesson when it's not our gift to teach the lesson.

Fear can be a good thing for you and me when it makes us afraid to turn our backs on the Lord.

Fear can be a good thing for you and me when it makes us afraid to deny the Lord before our fellow man.

Fear can be a good thing for you and me when it makes us afraid to not share Jesus with others.

Fear can be a good thing for you and me when it makes us afraid to willfully sin against the Lord.

Fear can be a good thing for you and me when it makes us afraid to not keep God's Commandments.

Fear can be a good thing for you and me when it makes us afraid to not help someone in need.

Fear is not always a bad thing, but many people believe that fear is always a bad thing.

There is a good kind of fear that adds more years to our lives.

Fear can be a good thing for you and me when it makes us afraid to be lost in our sins.

Fear can be a good thing for you and me when it makes us afraid to die in our sins.

Fear can be a good thing for you and me when it makes us afraid to tell lies.

Fear can be a good thing for you and me when it makes us afraid to not love the Lord.

Fear can be a good thing for you and me when it makes us afraid to not love our neighbors.

There are no sins in a good kind of fear.

A good kind of fear will give us peace of mind.

A good kind of fear will never cause us to tremble.

A good kind of fear will cause us to run away from trouble.

Fear can be a good thing for you and me when it makes us afraid to not spread the Gospel of Jesus Christ to all the world.

Many People Don't Believe

Many people don't believe that the Lord can help them.

Many people don't believe that the Lord can provide for them.

Many people don't believe that the Lord can heal them.

Many people don't believe that the Lord can open doors for them.

Many people don't believe that the Lord can make a way out of no way for them.

Many people don't believe that the Lord can supply all of their needs.

Many people don't believe that the Lord can do anything but fail.

Many people don't believe that the Lord is in control of the present.

Many people don't believe that the Lord is in control of the future.

Many people don't believe that the Lord was in control of the past.

Many people don't believe that the Lord can add many years to their lives.

Many people don't believe that the Lord can bless them with a good healthcare provider to take care of them when they get old and can't take care of themselves.

Many people don't believe that the Lord is all-powerful.

Many people don't believe that the Lord can move obstacles out of their way.

Many people don't believe that the Lord can interrupt their plans to let them know that making plans without Him is not wise.

Many people don't believe that the Lord can do so much more than what they can do.

Many people don't believe that the Lord is wiser than them.

Many people don't believe that the Lord is smarter than them.

Many people don't believe that the Lord can see what they see.

Many people don't believe that the Lord can feel what they feel.

Many people don't believe that the Lord can solve their problems.

Many people don't believe that the Lord can work things out for them.

Many people don't believe that the Lord can protect them.

Many people don't believe that the Lord can bless them with a miracle in their lives.

If you and I don't believe what the Lord can do for us, then we are truly spiritually dead and would probably be better off having never been born.

Higher

There is a higher power and that is God's power.

There is a higher wisdom and that is God's will.

There is a higher knowledge and that is God, who is all-knowing.

There is a higher mystery and that is that God sometimes works in mysterious ways.

There is a higher word and that is God's holy word.

There is a higher answer and that is God's answer to our prayers.

There is a higher peace and that is God's peace that He gives to his faithful.

There is a higher question and that is God's question and no one can answer it.

There is a higher mountain and that is God's mountain that Lucifer could not climb.

There is a higher star and that is God's star that sparkles throughout eternity.

There is a higher doctor and that is God, who heals our broken spirits.

There is a higher law and that is the holy law of God.

There is a higher judge and that is God, whose verdict cannot be overturned by anyone.

There is a higher surgeon and that is God, who operates on our motives and intentions.

There is a higher builder and that is God, who built the heavens, the earth, and the universes.

There is a higher architect and that is God, who designed the sun, moon, stars and the outer space with perfect measurements.

There is a higher government and that is God's government in heaven.

There is a higher love and that is God's love that was so great that He gave to us His only begotten Son so that whosoever believes in Him shall not perish but have everlasting life.

There is a higher education and that is from God's education to teach us with spiritual gifts to win souls to Him and build up His church.

There is a higher road that leads us to God, who has no dead ends for us and will not keep us from getting to our destination in heaven with Him.

That higher road is Jesus Christ, our Lord.

There is Something New to Learn

As long as we live, there is something new to learn in this world.

No one knows everything except the Lord, who will show us forevermore new things when we go with Him to Heaven one day when He comes back again.

I can learn something new about myself.

You can learn something new about yourself.

It takes time to learn something about someone, especially to learn something new about someone.

Someone you know may say something that you believed he or she would never say.

Someone you know may do something that you believed he or she would never do and you learn something new about him or her.

You and I don't always know what we will say before we say it.

You and I don't always know what we will do before we do it and learn something new about ourselves.

You and I don't always know what we will think before we think it.

You and I don't always know what we will feel in our hearts before we feel what's there.

That shows that we can always learn something new about ourselves.

You and I can learn something new about the Lord when we read His holy word.

The Lord can show us something new about Him that we need to know.

God's holy word is full of new revelations to help us learn something new about Him and about ourselves.

We can learn something new about how we should live our lives according to God's holy word.

We can learn something new about how we should treat one another according to God's holy word.

We can learn something new about how we should talk to one another according to God's holy word.

We can learn something new about the tricks of the devil according to God's holy word.

You and I can never get enough of learning something new as long as we live in a world where there is so much more to learn, especially about the Lord Jesus Christ.

Jesus knows all things in heaven and here on earth and throughout other worlds in countless universes.

When we get to heaven one day and live on the new earth, we will forevermore learn new things that will blow our minds.

Learning something new is eternal in Jesus Christ, our Lord and Savior.

We can never learn enough about Jesus, who knows the height, width, length, and depth of eternity that has no end in Him.

It's Easy to Think About

It's easy to think about people who don't support you for doing the good things that you do, but you can be thankful unto the Lord for the people who do support you for the good things that you do.

It's easy to think about people who don't call you on the phone to see how you are doing, but you can be thankful unto the Lord for the people who do call you on the phone to see how you are doing.

It's easy to think about the bad things that happened to you in your life, but you can be thankful unto the Lord for allowing some good things to happen in your life too.

It's easy to think about the mistakes that you made in your life, but you can be thankful unto the Lord for helping you to do something right in your life.

It's easy to think about what you should have done in your life, but you can be thankful unto the Lord for helping you to do good things today.

It's easy to think about how you failed in some things in your life, but you can be thankful unto the Lord for helping you to get the victory over things in your life today.

It's easy to think about what you didn't know in your life, but you can be thankful unto the Lord for allowing you to know what you need to know today.

It's easy to think about the people who let you down, but you can be thankful unto the Lord for the people who didn't let you down when you needed them.

It's easy to think about the people who did you wrong, but you can be thankful unto the Lord for the people who do you right today.

It's easy to think about the people who told lies about you, but you can be thankful unto the Lord for the people who told the truth about you today.

It's easy to think about people who don't care anything about your dreams, but you can be thankful unto the Lord for the people who are a part of your dreams.

It's easy to think about the people who don't love you, but you can be thankful unto the Lord for the people who love you today.

It's easy to think about the people who rejected you, but you can be thankful unto the Lord for the people who accept you for who you are today.

It's easy to think about the people who did bad things to you, but you can be thankful unto the Lord for the people who were good to you.

It's easy to think about the people who are your enemies, but you can be thankful unto the Lord for the people who are your friends.

It's easy to think about the people who have bad opinions about you, but you can be thankful unto the Lord for the people who have good opinions about you.

It's easy to think about the people who hate you, but you can be thankful unto the Lord for the people who respect you.

You and I can always be thankful unto the Lord, whose goodness outweighs the bad things in this sinful world.

To Tell Everything

It's not good to tell everything to people who may very well judge you for telling them everything on your mind.

It's not good to tell everything to people who made very well think badly about you for telling them everything on your mind.

It's not good to tell everything to people who may very well use it against you because you tell them everything on your mind.

It's not good to tell everything to people who may very well turn against you for telling them everything on your mind.

It's not good to tell everything to people who may very well throw it back in your face because you told them everything on your mind.

It's not good to tell everything to people who may very well look down on you for telling them everything on your mind.

It's not good to tell everything to people who may very well talk badly about you for telling them everything on your mind.

It's not good to tell everything to people who may very well want to have nothing to do with you because you told them everything on your mind.

Jesus Christ, our Lord and Savior, is the only one you and I can tell everything to, and it will always stay with Him.

You can tell everything to Jesus, because He will truly understand every word you say.

You can tell everything to Jesus, because He won't look down on you.

You can tell everything to Jesus because He won't turn His back on you.

You can tell everything to Jesus because He won't throw it back in your face.

You can tell everything to Jesus because He won't use it against you.

You can tell everything to Jesus because He won't criticize you.

The best of people can mean you and me good and well, but it's not good for you and me to tell everything to people who have sinned and fallen short of the glory of God.

There are some things that you can only tell to Jesus Christ, because He knows your mind and heart forevermore better than you and anyone else ever can.

Jesus knew everything on your mind before you were born.

Jesus knew everything you would say before you were born.

Jesus knew everything you would do before you were born.

Jesus knew your heart before you were born.

You can tell everything to Jesus and not ever have to think twice about it.

You can tell everything to Jesus and you don't ever have to feel bad about telling Him everything on your mind.

You can always feel good about telling Jesus everything.

You and I will never regret it if we tell Jesus everything on our minds, because He already knows.

If you and I tell people everything on our minds, they may not know how to take it all in.

Jesus knows how to take it all in every day.

We Can Limp Spiritually

We know that a pain in our leg or foot can cause us to limp when we walk.

Even a dog will limp if his or her foot is in pain.

A heartache can cause you and me to limp emotionally.

Grief can cause you and me to limp emotionally.

If someone tells lies about you and me, it can cause us to limp emotionally.

Heartache can cause us emotional pain.

Grief and causes emotional pain.

If someone tells lies about you or me, it can cause us emotional pain.

We know that limping is a sign of physical pain in our leg or foot.

Limping will surely slow you and me down, especially from walking too fast.

Deception can cause you and me to limp spiritually.

Not putting all of our trust in the Lord can cause us to limp spiritually.

If we disobey the Lord, it can cause you and me to limp spiritually.

We can limp physically, and in a few days or weeks the pain can go away.

We can limp emotionally, and it may take some months and years for the emotional pain to go away.

We can limp spiritually, and only the Lord can take away our spiritual pain that we have brought upon ourselves because we have turned away from Him.

We will normally feel physical pain that causes us to limp on one foot.

We would normally feel the emotional pain that gives us sorrow and even anger.

We don't normally feel spiritual pain until we get very ill and call on the name of the Lord to forgive us of our sins and repent in the hopes that the Lord will heal us and bring us back to wellness.

We can spiritually limp and not feel the spiritual pain for a very long time.

We can be so selfish in some ways and can be set in our own selfish ways and not know that we are limping spiritually.

Jacob limped on one foot when the Lord knocked his hip joint out of place.

Jacob had felt the pain that caused him to limp on one foot for no-telling how long.

Jacob probably didn't realize that he was limping spiritually before the Lord caused him to limp physically.

Jacob felt the physical pain when he might not have felt the spiritual pain for not putting all of his trust in the Lord to deceive his father Isaac.

Jacob limped emotionally and felt the emotional pain of believing that his brother Esau was going to kill him for stealing his birthright.

Limping spiritually is the worst kind of limp, because we won't feel the spiritual pain unless the Holy Spirit convinces us to repent of our sins unto the Lord, who sees us spiritually limping while we might not feel it.

If You Know It All

If you know it all, would it be a good thing in this sinful world?

If you know it all, you might very well get filled with pride.

There are people who are very knowledgeable about a lot of things, and many of them are filled with pride.

If you know everything in this sinful world, there may very well be some people who would want to kidnap you and hold you for a big ransom of money.

If you know everything in this sinful world, there are people who would want to worship you as if you were God.

If you know everything in this sinful world, there are people who would want to kill you for knowing their secrets.

If you know it all in this sinful world, it can surely bring so much trouble your way.

If you know it all in this sinful world, you may not get a good night's sleep and you may have many sleepless nights.

Why would you want to know it all in this sinful world where you would feel so all alone for knowing everything?

Can you ever imagine telling others everything that you know and having them take it all in?

If you were all-knowing in this sinful world, there are people who wouldn't trust you at all.

If you are all-knowing, there are people who wouldn't want to live anywhere near you.

If people knew that you knew all of their business, they would feel so very uncomfortable around you.

If people realized that you knew all of their thoughts, they would be afraid to be around you.

If people realized that you knew everything in their hearts, they would want to hide away from you.

You and I can be so thankful that only the Lord knows it all, even though we don't think about trying to hide away from Him.

We surely can't ever hide away from the Lord.

Only the Lord is all-knowing and no one can kidnap Him and hold Him for a big ransom of money.

Because of the sinful nature of this world, there are so many people who are not afraid to sin against the Lord, who is all-knowing and always brings the light to the darkness.

I Had Completely Forgotten

I have two little house dogs that I let outside in the fenced-in backyard.

One day in the late afternoon, I was upstairs in my townhouse talking on the phone.

I talked on the phone until it got dark outside.

As I was talking on the phone, I heard my little girl dog barking.

I paid her no mind, because I thought that she was barking because she heard some noise outside.

As I continued to talk on the phone, my little girl dog kept on barking.

I just didn't pay any attention to her as I talked on the phone for about two hours.

Then I heard someone knock on my front door while my dog was barking, so I walked down the stairs and looked out my kitchen window.

I saw my next-door neighbor standing in my front yard as his wife knocked on my door.

I turned on my front porch light and then I opened the door.

That young woman told me that she had heard my dog barking a lot and she thought that something was wrong.

She asked me if I was all right.

I told her that I was all right, and then I thanked her for checking on me.

After I closed the door, I went to check on my two little dogs that I thought were in their kennels.

When I looked in the kennels, I saw only one of my little dogs.

I figured out right away that my little girl dog was barking a lot because my little boy dog was outside in the backyard.

I had forgotten that I let him outside in the cold weather.

When I finally let him in the house, he was so happy to come back inside.

My little boy dog has a loud bark and I didn't hear him bark at all during the whole time that he was outside in the backyard.

I truly thank the Lord that he has a fur coat that kept him from getting too cold.

Sometimes, we can completely forget some things, but the Lord is so good and merciful that He will not make us regret it if it's in His will.

Some people have completely forgotten something and it caused some fatalities.

We just can't know why God allows a baby to be left in a hot car to die because a parent completely forgot to take the baby out of the car.

We can't question God and blame God when bad things happen.

Will One Day Be Immortal

You and I will one day be immortal for being saved in Jesus Christ, who lived a sinless life and died for our sins to save us from our sins.

He rose from the grave with the victory over death to give you and me eternal life when He comes back again on the clouds of glory with all the angels.

Jesus will one day give us an immortal body.

We will never need to shower or bathe ever again.

We will have no more bad breath ever again.

We will need no underarm deodorant ever again.

We will have perfect bodies.

We won't need haircuts or hairspray.

We will need no eyeglasses or eye drops ever again.

We will have perfect eyesight.

We won't need to get married.

There will be no marriages in heaven.

We won't need to have sex ever again.

You and I will one day have an immortal body that Jesus will give to us for being saved in Him.

We will eat from the Tree of Life.

We won't need to eat meat.

The fruit from the Tree of Life will be our meat to eat.

We will never get sick ever again.

We will never shed another tear ever again.

We will never get tired ever again.

We will never need to sleep ever again.

We will have a perfect memory.

We will never forget anything.

We will never get headaches ever again.

We will never get a toothache ever again.

Our teeth will never decay.

We will have never have dry skin ever again.

All who receive eternal life will have a perfect body and mind.

We will have no illness ever again.

We will have no back pain ever again.

We will have no knee pain ever again.

We will have no body pains ever again.

We will be young forever and ever.

We will have no gray hair ever again.

We will have no wrinkles ever again.

We will have no moles ever again.

We will have no freckles ever again.

We will need no bowel movements ever again.

The food in our stomachs will vanish away into nothing.

Jesus will one day give you and me and an immortal body that will be perfect without sin.

We will have no need to even urinate ever again.

There will be no spitting out saliva in heaven.

We won't need toilets in heaven.

We won't be doing those things in heaven.

We won't be picking our noses or digging in our noses in our immortal bodies.

We won't be doing those things in heaven.

Nature Knows Our Black Struggles

The sun knows our black struggles and shines down on black lives day after day.

Black love is always eye-catching to Nature that loves to give us black people peace of mind.

The sunlight will radiate it's light all around our black presence, with loyalty to us.

The sun knows our black struggles and rises and sets on our black lives that also matter.

Nature knew the struggles of our black ancestors during the four hundred years of slavery.

The mysterious full white moonlight knows our black struggles and glows so mysteriously down on our black uniqueness.

The full white moonlight will glow its mystic rays all around on our black courage to help us face up to biased people who hate us because of the color of our skin.

The full white moonlight glowed its beautiful light all around on our black ancestors, encouraging them to be bold enough to travel through the night on their way to the north with the moon's light illuminating their path.

All the stars know our black struggles and sparkle down on black dreams as they smile at us with hope.

The stars sparkled down on our black ancestors to let them know that they were embarking on a better day when they would be free.

God created nature to gladly accept us black people, regardless of the sinful nature of human beings.

Nature shows no prejudice against us black people day after day.

Nature shows no partiality against us black people day after day.

The rainbows arch over our black struggles with beautiful colors to remind us that black women are beautiful in every skin complexion.

The beautiful rainbow is God's promise to us black people that He will not destroy this world by water, ever again.

The air knows our black struggles and doesn't discriminate against us, letting us breathe it in and out of our nostrils day after day and night after night.

The air didn't discriminate against our ancestors while many of them made their escape from the South to the North.

The raindrops know our black struggles and fall down on us black people who live in an opinionated land where we are judged by the color of our skin.

The pure white snowflakes know our black struggles and fall down on us black people whose perseverance in this world is pure like the white snowflakes.

Our ancestors didn't do anything so wrong to be put in captivity and sent into slavery.

They were pure like the white snowflakes in their innocence.

God's motives are pure to let us black people exist from the beginning to the end of this world.

The puffy white clouds know our black struggles and puff up with loving and obeying the Lord.

The beautiful green grass knows our black struggles and lets us black people walk on it with dignity every day.

There is no green light shining over the brown grass of injustice, inequality, and prejudice towards us black people.

The beautiful tall trees know our black struggles and give us their shade and good things to look forward to.

The beautiful trees never wanted to use their limbs to hang any of our black ancestors.

The trees are very sorrowful and truly regret the hangings of the many black men, but there was no remorse in the hearts of many haters of us black people.

The mountains know our black struggles and give us mountaintop experiences of achieving our civil rights goals.

Martin Luther King Jr. saw the mountaintop of a much better life for us black people today.

The ocean waters know our black struggles and refused to swallow down all of our black ancestors in their great depths.

The ocean waters brought many of our ancestors safely over to a land of lies and deceptions that they encountered when they crossed over the ocean waters in ships of captivity.

The ocean waters have marveled at our black ancestors' boldness in accepting a new life of uncertainty in a new land that they would make great by their sweat, hard work, and tears of hope for better days to come to them.

Nature wrote our ancestors' names down in its book for the angels and for you and me to read and know that God was for our black ancestors and not against them.

The early morning fog knew our black struggles and kept many of our ancestors from being captured and sent back to their brutal slave masters.

The dense fog was the camouflage for our ancestors to escape with some peace of mind.

The deep forest sang some songs of victory to our black ancestors, who had to keep their voices down in the deep woods so that no adversary would hear their joy of one day being free.

The sacred ponds know our black struggles, and the ponds gave many of our ancestors some peace as they rested their tired bodies by the sacred waters.

The sacred ponds ministered to their souls about God's amazing love for them.

Nature knows our black struggles every day that nature gives us black people its complete trust, knowing that we will reach our full potential and make this world a better place to live in.

Nature is a gift to us from God, who hung the full white moonlight in the midnight with tears of joy for us black people to prosper in America.

Many of our black ancestors prayed to our Lord and Savior Jesus Christ under the full white moonlight that glowed its bright deliverance upon them.

They prayed in the early morning sunlight and knew that they would rise like the sun in their dreams of being free.

They prayed under the sunset and knew that their descendants would one day rise like the sun and get a good education in this nation.

Our black ancestors prayed to the Lord under all the stars sparkling in the night, and they knew that the stars of time would hug and kiss their visions of freedom from the oppression of slavery.

God used nature to reveal to our ancestors a much better life for generations of their descendants.

Today we know that our black ancestors' hopes, visions, and dreams were not in vain.

The Lord has brought us black people a mighty long way from then to today.

Our black presence has been here for thousands of years.

The Lord has brought us black people so very far and we still have far to go, which even nature would admit.

Nature is also a witness to the police brutality and killing of many young black men who don't get any justice because of haters hating on them every day.

Nature can only stand by and watch all of the injustice crushing down on us black people, but God is still on His holy throne getting justice to many of our black people who nature loves to be a good friend to every day.

Nature loves us black people, just like nature loves every other race people.

Nature has never defamed our black existence here in this world where our haters have defamed our black existence and will be held accountable to God on Judgment Day.

The beautiful flowers know our black struggles.

The beautiful flowers comforted many of our black ancestors who took some time out to smell the red roses meaning them good and well on their long journey to the north side of this nation.

The beautiful flowers rescued our ancestors from a lot of mental suffering when they worried about getting caught and taken back to their slave masters who they ran away from for very good reasons.

The beautiful flowers were on their pathway to a beautiful recovery from their adversary's thorns and the dried up weeds of their prejudice and hatred.

Nature knows our black struggles and reminds us that our sinful nature is not to blame for our haters to hate on us.

Their sins of prejudice and hatred are not our sins.

They can't blame us black people for their wrong doings.

God will hold prejudiced people accountable for their sins of hatred that even nature won't accept, for if it did it would lose all of its beauty and glory from God.

The universe knows our black struggles and understands that we black people are victimized by racism every day.

The universe is embarrassed to put up with a world filled with biased people who surely are not representing God who is love and loves everybody no matter the color of their skin.

Poetry About the Lord

Poetry about the Lord can give you and me a clear mind about what is really going on in this world.

Poetry about the Lord can take us up to spiritual heights and down to spiritual depths in the Lord.

The poetry that King David wrote in the Bible will take us up to spiritual heights and down to spiritual depths in the Lord.

Poetry about the Lord can bring out the real you and me in our hearts.

Writing poetry about the Lord can take our minds to Heavenly places.

It can take our minds to where our bodies can't go.

Poetry about the Lord can cause our hearts to wander off to the unknown that the Lord makes known to us.

Poetry about the Lord gives us favor with the wonders of time that will obey the Lord and wait kindly on anyone to read poetry about the Lord and be blessed.

Poetry about the Lord is a very inspiring language for Christian poets to speak to every race, creed, and culture who seeks the Lord.

This world has its troubles but poetry about the Lord can soothe troubled minds.

This world has its misery but poetry about the Lord can cheer many people up.

This world has its heartaches but poetry about the Lord can ease the heartaches of many people.

This world has its brokenness but poetry about the Lord can mend many broken people.

This world has its deceptions but poetry about the Lord can reveal the truth to many people.

This world has its darkness but poetry about the Lord can shine through many dark minds.

This world has its grief but poetry about the Lord can give some joy to many grieving people.

This world has its uncertainty but poetry about the Lord can cause many people to be certain about the Lord.

This world has its unpredictability, but poetry about the Lord is in line with God's word to protect many souls and save them.

Poetry about the Lord will make the most beautiful songs that you and I can never listen to.

Poetry about the Lord can cause an unbeliever to lay down his or her selfish ways and turn to the Lord.

Poetry about the Lord can help you and me grow stronger in the Lord.

Out of Our Comfort Zone

Sometimes, the Lord will take you and me out of our comfort zone, where we feel so safe day after day.

The Lord will sometimes put it on our hearts to knock on some of our neighbor's doors to give tell them something good about the Lord.

They may accept or reject what we want to tell them about the Lord.

We may sometimes feel uncomfortable about knocking on our neighbor's doors to share our faith in the Lord with them.

Sometimes, the Lord will take you and me out of our comfort zone to share a testimony about what the Lord has brought us through.

The Lord will put it on our hearts to give a testimony from the tip of our tongue or to write it down and get it published in a book.

We may feel uncomfortable about doing that, but we must do what the Lord wants us to do to glorify His holy name.

Sometimes, the Lord will take you and me out of our comfort zone to make us much stronger in Him.

The Lord may put it on our hearts to step on people's toes with the truth that they may not want to hear.

You and I may feel uncomfortable about doing that, especially when we know that they will reject the truth.

Doing things out of our comfort zone may not feel like a good experience, but the Lord will bless you and me for going out of our comfort zone for His holy name sake.

Sometimes, the Lord will take you and me out of our comfort zone to win souls to Him.

You and I must be willing to step out of our comfort zone to help someone hold onto the Lord when he or she may feel like turning their back on the Lord.

The Lord knows that if you and I stay in our comfort zones all the time, we will have no spiritual growth so we can be more like Him.

Sometimes, the Lord will take you and me out of our comfort zone and we should be glad that He will do that because it lets us know that doing His holy will is not always a comfortable thing but it's always a good thing for us whose will has no salvation.

Doing our own will can make us feel so comfortable and will cause us to lose our souls. Sometimes, the Lord will take you and me out of our comfort zone so that we can open up and share some of our bad experiences with people who need to know that we will give the Lord the glory and praise for sparing our lives as we went through those bad experiences.

When the Lord takes you and me out of our comfort zone it's always for His holy purpose, and we won't understand what that is until the Lord reveals His purpose to us.

We must have faith in the Lord, who always knows what is good for us.

You and I don't like to come out of our comfort zone because it feels so good to be comfortable all the time.

Sometimes, the Lord will take you and me out of our comfort zone to let us know that our lives are all about Him and not about us.

The Lord created us to live for Him, and not to live for ourselves day after day.

www.ingramcontent.com/pod-product-compliance
Lightning Source LLC
Chambersburg PA
CBHW070122080526
44586CB00013B/1354